A Beginning In Smiles,
An Ending In Tears

A Beginning In Smiles, An Ending In Tears

Christian Powell

authorHOUSE®

AuthorHouse™ LLC
1663 Liberty Drive
Bloomington, IN 47403
www.authorhouse.com
Phone: 1-800-839-8640

Published by AuthorHouse   12/17/2013

ISBN: 978-1-4918-4319-2 (sc)
ISBN: 978-1-4918-4477-9 (e)

Library of Congress Control Number: 2013923109

Contents

Knot

In the soil laid a small seed where the roots begins to grow, leaves of bright green colors reach the sky all on it's own.

After seasons of many rainfalls and bright sunny days, a tree of many branches stands where that one small seed did lay.

But there's a knot in the tree trunk where a branch grew out so strong, a reminder of a once mighty bough, which has taken a fall.

The sap surrounds it, as the bark tends to heal its open wound, and the branch just lay's there dying, on the ground of morning dew.

Mighty branch, you held such promise, you were strong and fairly long, but now you just lay torn and strewn upon the ground as a log.

Though the tree has many boughs, as it sways braced against the breeze, new rings grow in its trunk each season, growing and shedding all sorts of colorful leaves.

Mighty branch, you held such promise, you were strong and fairly long, but now you just lay torn and strewn upon the ground as a log.

So now the knot, it heals yearly, like the branch really wasn't there, just a part of the tree bark, a weakness it hardly bears.

On the ground where it's dead branch, lies now almost completely gone, decaying and rotting, providing new soil as the years continue going on and on

A Honey would

Happy Birthday Jesus, on this Christmas Day

Thank you for your blessings. These past 2000 years and days

The Son of God, we championed and make our lives

Seem to be with you, for you, for ourselves

You showed us the ultimate of Love, dying on that cross

And for us that believe, we prepare the

Day you come back

Oh Happy Birthday, Jesus on this Christmas Day

An Empty Picnic Basket

I have an empty picnic basket
Just sitting ready on the shelf
It's here all clean and neat as can be
All alone here with me here in my room by myself
I'm sitting alone thinking of you
Wondering why you an I aren't enjoying
Nice weather, fine music and times
But all there's here
Is an empty picnic basket, all-alone with me here in my room
Neatly folded is my blanket, plaid in blue, like I love you
Wanting to be out on a meadow, where you and I
Can gaze at the sky

And I can look into your eyes of blue while you look into my eyes, too!

As one

We are one, we are one in mind

And as one, in love, as one, we'll always hug.

Life of one, from one of our lives together

One is us and of us is one (or two)

Love is one we share, and love shows to all

As one we care. As one we ourselves

As no one, or any one lives this one love

And as any one can see, this one is the one

To one another, as one surely knows, that one

Way or the other, this one will be the true one

Before

Before, during and after

Past present and future

I will, I shall, I did

Long ago, presently, and for ever more

Till I'm done with all of it

Behind The Red Door

Our view of early horizon stretches long and even, blending in the contours of the trees,

The misty clouds of this morning bring my lover's embrace close to me. Stars of nighttime fade to faint light now, wisps of fragrant breezes fill crispy fresh cold air. Turning from the mirror as I finish shaving, I give her a gentle loving stare.

Out of this billowing darkness, sits a small cottage set on a hill, filled with love and surrounded by gardens, a creek's waterfall flows over rocks gurgling steady as it spills. Looking out of their picture window, having had fried eggs and some toast, they settle to a cup of coffee, he finishes his early morning smoke. Behind the red door of their small home, guitar music can gentle be heard, they get ready to start on their journey, he gathers his key's, she her purse.

Rays of appearing sunshine, reach up to the sky as our world turns , reaching out through fading darkness, brightening lands farmers have plowed into furls.

Trees give way to large sprawling meadows, under oak , ash trees and palms, orchards have started to bloom with their flowers, filling branches, of apples, peaches and cherries, to be ready to reap for us all.

Out parked on our fresh paved new driveway, our convertible sit's ready to go, I pick up my briefcase and lunch box, kiss my wife and I head out the door. She follows behind him to step out, turning a lock on that red door securely, she breathes in the mornings fresh air, I open her door for my darling, she settles in as I turn down the street towards New Pilgrims Square.

Lurking down around the corner, waiting in a white panel van, two unsavory unkempt bearded fellow's, start to initiate their illegal plan.

They see that the couple have departed, they go to their door on a ruse, jimmying the lock with a crowbar, they enter and look around for valuable loot. Filling black bags with silver sets and jewelry, taking a few older paintings and goods. Stepping outside they look in both directions, closing the now splintered broken red door, they get in that white van and scoot.

Returning together from their long day, a day that has treated them well, a new contract for her in the making, he a new client who bought most of his manuals and books.

They both drive up that drive-way, freshly paved from the weekend before, and head out of the open convertible, to go in their home behind the undiscovered broken red door.

Inside they discover the carnage, the tumbled furniture spread all around, see the broken glass, the open jewelry box, and notice all that is missing, she gets on her cell phone and calls the cops. Reports are taken in earnest, insurance is given a list, he tells her it's all just material, and hugs her and gives her a kiss.

He lights a log in the fireplace, she settles in her favorite chair, a small glass of wine between them, behind the red door that has been repaired. And as for those two unsavory fellow, they just vanished into night times cool air.

Blue eyes

Blue eyes, that look up toward the sky

Makes my teeth smile, smile for a long, longest time.
I smile & looking up to the sky with my eyes

I like saying your name and hear you, love, say mine.

My eyes glance up in the sky,
my teeth & cheeks smile, you make me feel like no other guy.

And know what darts my eyes to maybe look into

The sky, you've made me feel you like my company

Every time you say my name, it leaves me

Warm to tell you, your name makes me smile

These times go by quickly gone the next

Sounds in our ears, when we get near

I like saying your name. (it makes me smile)
Love

I like saying it in a charming way

It makes me look up, and smile a smile hoped to be shared

You taught me to say yours and I showed

You how I like mine being said, I hope like me

It makes you smile

Bobby D

Bound & shackled down
Got me hangin' on the ground

I can't lift my head just to see
Proud to have Bob Dylan call you friend from the stage
So gratefully to me as I please

Build a bridge (get over it)
10/22/13 6:19 AM

Life for me was going along so well

It never did take that long

A hop over that small creek as far as I could tell

Till I met you and things were going pleasantly strong

I never felt things would go tragically wrong

The divide of that stream started to deepen the chock

It feel's like someone hammering a wedge around the clock

the currants of the flowing water kept growing so fast

I just couldn't believe what had happened in our past

Till those still waters flowed around in a rage

The deeper the canyon and gap had arranged

Now crossing that water was difficult at best

I need to make certain it ends now I guess

I found a few planks and big boulders and rocks

And built a bridge over that gorge using these building blocks

I travel it now, it is easy again

It's a walk down the road, I move on ahead

I built a bridge to get over it, To go down that road

Times are much easier and I forget, I don't carry that load

That bridge is now simple, not as difficult or hard,

Level thinking and sturdiness gives me some peace with no alarm.

Bundle of sticks

A fresh garden blossom of fine colored roses

Thorns and green leafs below spread swirls of dark soft red pedals

Angle cuts below set in crystal mirrored water filled vases

For days the fragrance and beauty abides

To sparkle in sunlight grace the sideboard near the table

To be replaced by just a memory or a thoughtful light jape

Drying though watered, the fading wilt brings bereavement now set aside

Out in the rubbish pile, a bundle of sticks is all that is left

Checking the mail box late Sunday night

It's been a long road, driving down this highways winding path
To end up in this town, his journey's final act
As he sets up his new home, near the place where they once owned
he still wonder's why, you left him like you did.

He's been waiting for a call, he longs to hear it ring,
Or dial you up to talk, but your number's out of reach
Is their something wrong with him, did he stumble or did he fall
he want's to hear from you, to an answer his curiosity once and for all.

So now he goes out to the street,
to get a glance of something to give him ease
to let go of his past
his empty hopes fades and are quickly dashed.

He acts like he is crazy
Searching out in hopes that maybe
She's reconsidered, and wants him, it's all been a mistake

Checking the mail box late Sunday night
for a letter he knows she'll never write
to get a second chance,
to start a renewed romance
and receiving a letter from her, to send him in so many words
saying she misses him and wants to come back

He won't get any mail
it's silly of him to fail
to seek a written word,
from you he just hasn't heard.
No communication, it's like he's been cut off

He puts his hands in the pockets of his pants
Returns to his apartment to let the hours pass
Hiding so the world
won't see him cry

Sitting at his cardboard box table
Just wishing he was able
To hear the soothing comfort of her soft familiar voice
As he shuffles through their photo's
Of old memories of a relationship, now disabled
All his Wedding pictures that has broken him up deep inside.

He wonders if he'll ever hold her in his arms again
Those thoughts still run over and over in his head
To reminisce of embraces of love.

But as the weekend ends, night finds him heading out again,
Checking the mail box late Sunday night,
For a letter he knows she'll never write
To get a second chance
To start a renewed romance
But he knows that he will never receive a letter from her to be read.

Clouds

Clouds all white are covering all of the sky

Clouds, sometimes you are just one puffy glob

Will you be way up or grouped in layers

Clouds, sometimes you are not even around

With the wind blowing you under the other mix a shape

Of varying shades of gray

Now it looks like it's starting to rain

Up here, this could go on for days

Clouds, sometimes, I'm so happy and feeling so good

Tomorrow night you're covered in colors of pink,

orange purple, yellow through streaks of blue

but I know that soon you'll darken and fade into black

Clouds, sometimes I think these sooth my head

Or on the finish
or just caught up in one
to resume

Clown

Reflections of a mirror, sunlight shining from my cup,
musings of my mind make me look back to what I had once
Is it bright like that sunshine, or cluttered dull from hopes that fade?
Is it just a positive buffed up version, or has it just been rearranged?
My 20/20 version is stilted, my recollection is somewhat skewed
Mixed in with hopeful wishes, filled with dreams never to come true
No, my mind now thinks more clearly, the truth is much plainer to me
You took another direction, it all becomes clearer looking back as it
seems

What we once thought was the right way for a path to be taken
What that direction could possibly hold
Is a path that has left me wondering, and sees you wandering down a
different road.

You used your effort to plan ahead quite clearly
You used you effort to go down this path
Never using your energy to make things better
Just ready to move on with your life so fast

Not using your talent or love to stay together,
Rejoining was not in your plans
Spoke to anyone but me who would listen
Like a hot potato you dropped me, refusing to ever take a moment to
look back.
No more touching each other in wonder, no more affection of holding
our hands
No more loving embraces of lusting, no more landing in a sweat on our
bed
No more talking of future finances, no more talking about having kids,
no more loving looks of discernments, no more hugging or kisses in our
midst.

But I didn't shut down as you might have hoped for, if you planned this
for me to break down.
I have other plans at this moment, since you no longer wish for me to
be around.

I like flirting with the ladies, there's so many to choose by leaps and
bounds
Hooking up with them gives me much pleasure,
Now to me, who looks like a clown?

Dropping me is a loss for you lady,
Letting me go was a mistake that you made,
The grass that you didn't take care of,
Going over that fence, you'll find aint so great

I hope you find someone better,
someone you can truly enjoy,
But when all of your problems return and haunt you,
I'll be laying on roses, having someone playing with me like a toy.

And if you should ever try calling me,
I'll be friendly and civil to you,
I don't have to be someone different,
changing all those things that I do.

Dumping me has become your misfortune
Dropping me was a selfish mistake
Wear your makeup and bright colored wig with your big shoes,
Just go lay in the bed that you made

Clues (to my blues)

I noticed your tilt, mirrors and seat are adjusted
No more givin' you jewels just to get next to you
Now I just wander, walkin' down the avenues

Our stations aren't there on the radio buttons
But I'll see what I can do, something I won't hesitate to use
I want to feel high, high as a big balloon in full flight the hows and the
whys

Your plugs are sparkin' for another and if this is true,
Goth nothin' else to do, cry my eyes at the moon
Not pounding the streets in these shoes, I think I got the news

I've got some clues to my blues, feeling misplaced and abused
I've got some clues to my blues, not like a toad stool in a dark damp
room.
Givin' me some clues to my blues, clues to my blues

Like so many empty bottles of booze, I'm losin' you.
The sound of spit in a spittoon, in an old saloon at high noon.
Givin' me the clues to my blues, I think I'm losing you.

Could be just a little bit happier

Could be just a little bit happier
I'm just ashamed; I don't want to lose my sanity
I'm not the better man; I've come to admit it
Sitting alone in a crowd and not knowing
Finally it's plain to see making matters worse
A little less happy
But I miss you, think about us both

And not sharing maybe one day, but caring all along

So as I see you and others

Clear where I see myself to others

I'm not the better man in this picture

I'm just barely

A single man who chose to be alone

Just try not to do any more denying or escaping

After 50 years now better start trying

To love away right now

Please let it begin

Who knows, you know?

I shall get on my knees and pray

Time will tell

Don't let the effect affect the way you feel

I'd like to wet your whistle before I get busy

But going on joking with witches, which I like,

Stops when I have to start depending on

These things there's a last time for everything

Like a parachute, it needs to work the 1st time

just as enforcement to damage control

But shore in up somehow, some way

You are right as rain

Empty box

I sent you a box in the mail, open it up now,
see how you showed your love to me,
it's filled with all sorts of goodies,
all of our hopes, plans and dreams.

I sent you all that you gave to me,
all the things you gave me in life.
That shows your love and affection,
to help us live our way as husband and wife.

The box I sent you is empty, like the love that
I came to receive, no letter or Bible, or silver cup,
no love or commitment to be seen.

So I hope you find it and wonder,
I'm so glad it arrived in the mail,
Just a big cardboard package that's empty,
with nothing in it, and with it, Our dreams.

I sent you a big empty package,
no roses or candy or card,
The box that you open is empty,
and you know that it's just like your heart.

So don't start calling or writing, or texting,
you have made your decision final to me,
an empty box that I sent you by mail,
is now full of the love given me.

Look around the box if you want to, it's not
full of paper but air,
Just like the comfort and help when we married dear,
just a package full of despair.

So I hope you find it and wonder,
I'm so glad it arrived in the mail,
Just a big cardboard package that's empty,
with nothing in it, except for our dreams
of which you don't care.

E,D,A,G,B,E

Everyone, drink a good beer, everyday

Believe in the dream, keep on now, believe it.

Together on the path, we walk and we laugh

Tomorrow will always have things uncompleted

And we will just go on believing

Everyone, drink a good beer everyday

Eyes of Potatoes

You cut up a potato, and plant it down in the dirt

And under blue skies the leaves grow so green.

And lots of them grow

As rain waters the soil

Potato eyes do your job

Lots of potatoes underground

Potato eyes, look all around

And watch lots of potatoes grow under the ground

Lovely eyes, a beautiful brown

Growing and growing under the ground

The season has really covered this fine acre

And has everyone talking and looking around

Where are these round spuds?

All oblong & round

Growing and growing, under the ground

To sprout new eyes of potatoes

To see a new season abound

Free flow

Free flow of independence to your spirits free will
Spoken or thought out will your path of agreement be,
Remember how graceful are you're moment's that thrill
In past passing movements felt so wonderful to me.

To touch sweaty strong arms on your shallow back sway ,
Smooth curves of knees towards your legs I caress,
Looking as your head from me turns slightly away,
Lovely hair and brown eyes mine eyes long to possess

We join and rock slowly to a rhythm unheard
Hips curved round soft in half circles.
Vibrate gently with ripples yet no sound or a word
A length of my spirit is round, full and encircled

Return yee to me from my dreams of this vision
To be warm all together in both safe to combust
Breaths of you drive me on my mission
This final ending explodes so robust

As the two of us fall on the sides of our shaking
A calm overtakes, our bodies untangle
Hold tightly yet gently in lasting depths of quaking
A short sleep or a rest under colorful quilt edges dangles

Fantastic

Fun & fantastic, sparkles glow on

This place of eternal beauty

We've all had dreams & prayers

Focused brightly in our minds, and each day,

as it goes by, we passionately add

Another piece and go back to whatever's at home

After, during and before, silence veils

The moment the sounds and visions dance

And abound

Let when we're together, holding each other

Close, it's as we've always been here, yes love

Like we have never been apart

We long to love forever, can give it it's all

We can, our smiles, eyes to eyes, and

Praise above, this never ends, will give us a

child

Fork In The Road

Got a big steak philly sandwich and I'm heading on out down the road
A large hot cup of cowboy coffee and two packs of camels as I go
Flamenco music playing loud on the CD and the gas tank is full
And I'm wearing my dark sunglasses and my window is slightly unrolled

Heading east I wonder how the traffic is as other drivers go by
For if they are just like me they know my cautions are always raised
high
It's a sunny day the wipers off, but I splash them a couple times
Wipe the bugs and dust off my windshield on my magic highway flight

Suddenly I spot a hitcher on the front side of the upcoming exit, blonde
and in her jeans and hand held out looking for someone in transit
She got an old back-pack on and doesn't look too mean, I see that she
is got on cowboy boots and cowgirl hat, and pulls her thumb up as she
gazes sharply with a keen eye towards me.

Easing off to the side of the road I stop and open the handle , she
takes her hair and tosses it back, closes the door and begins to
ramble
Thanks for stopping mister, I hear her starting to say
Are you going far out east or just past those hills . . . I say I'm going
all the way
she tells me cool, it really gives me the chills to see those trucks, I just
got out of one ,all he wanted to do is, well I told him to go to a slower
speed and drop me off, 'cause I wouldn't be that interested in having his
brand of lunch, I've been hiding from my ex for six years now, just had
enough, but you looked fine, I'm rather tired , really, thanks a bunch.

Dark asphalt pavement hummed the tires smoothly of my car, we wound around those hills and valleys up and down, rolling faster than Ramon Montoya's melodic fingering guitar. I was getting hungry now, gobbled half my sandwich and started to hear her snore, getting comfortable in the passenger recliner, me flicking my cigarette ashes out the door

I fumbled in my glove box for some smokes, I had a new pack to get, it'll be four hours till we get to a gas station, sleep away, we'll get there yet

Almost four hundred miles we traveled, until the dawn rose out of the night and her being started to come alive again to see this awesome sight

After two more smokes she was awake, and a roadside cafe brought us to a stop, resuming into sunlight after breakfast, that's when I noticed a fork in the road just slightly up ahead.

I asked her if she was continuing forward, as I was going to the right, she said no but thank you for everything she was going to the left. I'm glad we spent these moments, as you traveled down this road, and wish you all the happiness, I wished her well and continued to roll.

And in the rear view mirror, I see that she was content, to raise her thumb up boldly, to see what ride she'll get

Got a Clue to my Blues (version 2)

I go walking with you under the trees.
I confess I don't know you, I didn't see
Dreamin' of holdin' hands with me
We used to watch the sun on the rise
And watch it fall you and I sittin' in peace

(Chorus)
I've got a clue to my blues, I gotta
Clue to my blues,
I got a clue to my blues
I think I'm losing you

All my trunk of hopes and poems ,
Filled with dreams.
Now all don't mean that
Much to me.
I can't think of a time
You weren't here with me ,oh my
Keep on waiting, find another, it's not you
I got a clue to my blues to be with each other, it is so true
Good God woman, up to the heavens
Not wondering or worrying all the time
No one else instead
Change,
Your eyes and mine, flirting all the time
Your soft voice soothing my ear
How now do I go on from here?

(Chorus)
Sun go up. The sun go down, but
I thought you'd always be around

(End)
I got a clue . . .

Got Time?

Chris Powell? Or customer patron?

I get dopey, it's easy to tell

Who do I think you see or try to be?

I have my idea, at least, and give it a go

I spilled it out like it needed to be said

Got time, for me I mean,

Or should I now go, take my ass down the road

I really think I should go

Got Two Bucks?

Just row on over the river
Yes, just walk on over that bridge
That's where you'll find money
All the money you ever wanted and wished for
Go and get yourself fists full please, just get out of my mist

You can swim yourself through the river
or walk on over the bridge
Sail, row or paddle, keep that money forwarding your quest

If you want to know where there's mountains of gold
To fill your pockets with glee
Just row on across the river or just walk on over the bridge

Your eyes won't believe that money
like leaves are bundled and stacked neatly in rows
But please stop your begging from me
and please just go, would you please go?

To ask me for my last dollars, to say "got two bucks?" so easily
I understand how nice for you it is in asking
Yet to me two bucks is all I got to my name
To tell you the truth, it gives me a pain

So just row on over that river
Just walk on over the bridge
That's where you'll find money
And for you will fulfill your wish

Night Shadows

Hair stand on end!, Electric shock!
Crockagator lurking under logs!
The polka dot coat on the leopard poised to leap-
Making you lay flat on the floor

The darkness casts its shadow, pale light domes
Outlines you think all around
Oh I wish I had wood for the fireplace last night,
But now I can stoke a full load
New ember's burn bright, that lessens my fright
Of the night in the dark with no light
But we start a new day,
Everyone's has gone away
Until the shadow return's tomorrow night

Halloween

Clanging from the tower sounds precisely
As the clock strikes at ten o'clock
Late October's chilly air makes me tug and wrap
On my scary masquerades evening frock

This costume I have planned for this evening
Almost thought of it all through the week
To have fun on this outing with this outfit
With my painted face for Halloween

My sack is filled with goodies,
I know they aren't good for my teeth
Gathered up stashed and hidden under my pillow
To be eaten all thru the week

Later on this scary fright night
At the party my best friends have thrown
Gathering with other goblins
We are all thrilled right down to our bones

Bobbing for apples we laugh and act foolish
And share cups of dry ice filled Hawaiian punch
We eat popcorn balls that are sticky
And peanut brittle square caramel's crunch

Spooky music fills up this party
We dance to bright sparkling lights
Gazing out at the evening of darkness
Phantoms and monster's jig of delight

A witch's pointed hat and her broomstick
Walking dead zombies and bloody man wrapped up in gauze
Twins dressed like a giant orange pumpkin
And some fool dressed up as Santa Claus

Ending the night on a high note with smiles
Walking down the cobblestone streets
We hear bells from that tower hitting midnight
Kicking gathered up dried autumn leaves

Silver streaks of a cloud passes above us
Covering white moons bright reflecting light
We part to go back to reality
And dream of this wonderful Halloween night.

Have you ever been hurt by somebody?
11/12/13 11:57 PM

Have you ever been hurt by somebody?, like someone stepping on your toes?
Someone who makes you feel so badly, your heart feels heavy and the juices in your brain start to flow?

Wondering why they've hurt you, tears swell up in your eye, it hard to take a breath now, no love or comfort as you sigh.
You search your memory for reasons, no ideas come to your mind, curling up into a ball, seeking embraces and reasons why.

Come to me my darling, take the pain away from me, or have I hurt you so you have to go? It doesn't make any sense to me.
Don't leave me alone to wonder, don't make me think you don't care,
Give me the love I am seeking, give me the love that shows you're aware.

I need my loving partner, don't let me stay alone like this, after all we've been through, it's just to much to bear. Hold me close in warm embraces, give me your sweet and able lips, my body needs your involvement, some tender moments of unrequited bliss

We need some reconciliation, a reflection of our goals, memories of past fun, of laughter, moments of loves undying glow. Will you come to me my darling, hold me in your arms so tight, or leave me here to bury my head, alone with red eyes filled with tears as I cry?

I want to see your smile, your white bright shinning teeth, the rosiness of your cute and round, lovely upturned cheeks. And make me smile towards you, make my brain and mind feel clear, make my heart stop all of this wandering, because I love you my dear.

I'm empty now without you, you have left me on my own, what can I do but wonder, are you getting ready to go?
"I've been hurt before I've told you, you've assured me that you care, but your absents leaves me wondering, it leaves alone now feeling scared.
I'll go away without you, I'll leave this very day, I'm going back to my mother, this will be you I'll come to blame."

A intervention is called for, maybe some counseling for us both, for I fear this will lead us, to a splitting and parting of ways and loss of hope. "I have come to a decision, yes the end is now in sight, I can't get over my feelings, that you gave me during that fight. So I'll pack my bags and leave you, make you cry and sob on your own, make you sit and wonder darling, and ask for a divorce."

"Don't try to ask my forgiveness, I hear you coughing and breathing with your tears, no stringing along will I give you, no hopes of settling or rekindling, pleading or begging from you in my ears. I have decided to leave you forever, to find myself in this new found release, say we married to quickly without thinking, I hope I can find a new commitment to embrace."

So now I sit with my head in my hands wet, of all of these tears of mine that I cry, and wonder what the hell was she thinking, leaving me alone and saying good-bye.

Hope for the future

Harken the sound of birds in flight my love

Soft as their wings, fill my ears gentle from your lips whispers flow

Sunlight is shaded, filtered leaves keeps us cool in late afternoon splendor's glow

A gentle light breeze blow between your hairs curls and makes it flutter highlighting your expressions

Oh speak to me my love, it calls me close to you in flurry of pleasant intensions.

Your golden light skin, hanging bejeweled earrings falling and moving to your nods and view

Tantalizing red lips and curved eyebrow arch to highlight your hazel brown eyes, yes I love you my beautiful muse.

Speak to me my darling, murmur words lightly in the wind

Touch of my hand brings relief from your lovely tan colored soft skin

I gaze to you in wonder, sir, leather belt wrapped below your v-shaped chest

A brass band surround your upper arms of muscles, of which you've been thankfully blessed

The headband holds your mane of flowing blonde locks, strong cheekbones that highlights your bright smile that is slightly tilted, off cocked.

Pointed elbow hold your lyre strumming steady as you so lovely play

Hands of strength, fingers long, your sounds of music is full of grace

Brown laces around your calves hold your leather sandals upon your feet
Compared to my other lovers, you stand out and really don't compete
Deep low gentle voice, it inspires, brings a sparkle in your eyes
Charms those chirping birds down from the bright cloudless blue skies.

Golden necklace reflects through shaded sunlight, the wondrous colors of your blouse, smooth legs of tan, toe rings sparkle silver delight, I'm so glad that you're around
Your gentle expression in alluring tones touch me, like I hoped it would always be
Gives me hope for the future, giving hope of my night and daytime dreams.

Oh sir you excite me, you seduce me in so many ways,
Never have I been so taken, never have I been talked to this way.
Yes my lady of splendor, yes my lady of gentle soft tones,
Come with me to my valley, come and make for us a settled home.

We will dance to the sounds of the world,
We shall be sheltered from every storm
We shall raise many children, my darling, yes to us many children shall be born
So walk with me my companion, walk with me to the valley below
let us build a family in this meadow
let us make this house a loving filled home

How beautiful
the wind sounds
8/29/13 3:26 PM

Yolk yellow sun so bright, in hot day's of summer now passing, giving way to shorter brightness, during a night spending pleasantly together around the campfire, under the moon glow for some dancing.

How beautiful the wind sounds, blowing thru the tall trees so smooth,

raising noise gentle and harder, then suddenly stops, and resumes.

Tired blue skies washed with grey streaks with white puffs billow their way round, tossing and turning their shapes, the summer slowly passes, sunshine's bright light, is beginning to go down.

Autumn is hinting to the leaves, it's time to remove your green gowns.

Birds still are chirping, squirrels round up their nuts, the bees are flying to gathering nectar in the meadows in a rush of flowers clinging near the ground.

Rain lightly falls sparkling the grass in small droplets, plants have gone to seed, brambles of blackberry vines are flush, luscious fruit ripe in full goblets.

On the ground no leaves have fallen, none have left from limbs of full branches. Fruits have all grown fuller, some have yet to ripen.

Late flowers bloom in flourishing colors, adding delight to the day, while other plants have grown strong, knowing falls on it's way.

Dusty paths of small mammals now worn smooth among bushes, waiting for softer wet conditions to show with pads and claws they've imprinted along slug paths translucent.

Sticks and small branches, scattered in tangles, laying wind tossed all about from breezes of new seasons, cobwebs full in splendid patterns, catch bugs flying round to be wrapped up neatly, stored away to be eaten.

Warm days turn colder, there is a hush on the rise, with fall soon approaching, ducks and geese eye towards the south to soon take their long flight.

Oh, summer, what fine days you have given, bright skies at night to show the stars of blinking lights and meteors streaking. With you almost now over and giving way to the changes for the new season, days grow shorter, nights longer, spinning world on it's mission.

Wow

I can be coaxed if I go along
It sounds good like singing a song

Convince me, and tug on my sleeve
I will do anything you please

Yes?

I love you hearing beautiful music
I'd like to meet with you when you get off
I'd rather smile with you then go home alone & smoke these
Cigarettes
Sometimes it dawns on me
So make the answer yes, Please?

$

If you have enough money and you want
Something done
If you have enough money most likely it will be
The way it's done,
Until something of someone can out do, or pay to do things their
Own way.
Plump red juicy polka dotted strawberries
Slices on whip creamed biscuits stacked high in a bowl
All it takes to take the cake
Just is a bit of dough

Time

It's hard to go back, yet so easy to move forward
You know every time you do or show. Slips away faster, not seeming
To ever stop,
I'm just here, caught up in this flow

Drizzle

It's not that I'm sad to those who look on
A slow patter of rain drains the sky,
Although there's no movement, a head thru some mist
The wind moves the branches leaves a drip curling downward
But springs back with the gust, but it's sopping and chilly,
And i don't feel like smiling all that much
Oh make me happy, oh make me smile,
Bring cheer & laughter along with your grin
And as I gaze upon your eyes so lovely, warmth of your
Beauty, my cheeks get their exercise, imbibe it within

I'm Falling

Cliffs sharp cut edges, we stand looking outward, down beneath,
Gazing at the steep slopes, rocks and surf that's far below,
Standing near my side on our unsteady feet

We lean slightly backwards to safety from below,
we stand back wondering together,
Is this the end of our path,
Is this the "end of our rope?"

My voice lowers to a harking of critics' cringing advisements,
And grates your pink ears, lowers your soft rosy red cheeks.
It diminishes your sweet appearance
Sorrowful wrinkles cover your face as I get weak.

"Catch me" I say, as I start with my behavior,
Don't let harsh words of our experiences spoken down by lower phrases
Grip me tight by my hand
Lift me up and with positive glances.

Show me smiles of understanding,
thoughtful words, sparkling eyes,
Maybe just show me laying down on earth's green patches,
resting under the bright daytime skies.

For I'm starting to bring us down,
I'm beginning to stray,
I'm falling , please catch me, I can't go down this way.

With no words of kindness,
or no wise looks to my face,
I stumble, I trip, keep me back now,
keep me safe in this black place

For I feel like I'm falling,
out to those rocks down below
to be swept out by dark water,
crashing splattered on my landing
over this cliff I shall wander, I know.

But if you hold me real tight,
and don't let me go,
Our bond would be unyielding,
We could stand together; let it not take my soul.

Given Myself the Blues

I've given myself the blues, did it when it came to lovin' you

When I take in a breath, deep down in my chest

Tears just swell up in my eyes, yes my face
droops and I can't hide my mind

'cause the thought of not lovin' you . . . I've just given myself the blues

I've given myself the blues, yes I am sad, it's oh so true

And in my blank look, a stare of despair

When I look up, I still see you're not there

My mind keeps searching for clues,

sitting here just tapping my worn, leathery shoes

I've just given myself the blues

I've given myself the blues, from here on, I'll be just one of a few

To gaze by the road, just carrying that load

of someone, who has gotten bad news

I've just given myself the blues

I've given myself the blues, now what's there to do

Keep walking along, maybe sing an old song

Step along on my way, maybe find a new muse

I can only hope it is true

So I'll stop giving myself the blues

Jasper

Jasper, you were a lot similar to a man just like me,

Marring into this fine family,

A proud picture of you showed your pride,

Of attaching yourself to your bride.

An old tin-type I think it is called,

A portrait of you standing upright and tall

An old style beard on your face

A suit neatly worn with such grace

Oh Jasper, poor Jasper

I wish I could have warned you against your upcoming disaster

Oh Jasper, poor Jasper

Wedding into that fine family

Taken a hundred and fifty years ago

Back then that was just how it goes

I heard you died shortly after getting wed

Yes Jasper, I guess marring her made you dead

I just hope that my fate isn't the same

I divorced her to avoid an early grave.

Oh Jasper, poor Jasper,

I wish I could have warned you against your upcoming disaster

Oh Jasper, poor Jasper,

Wedding into that fine family

Jennifer

Jennifer, with the green-blue eyes
Trying to get along with her life,
Am I just a step to get out of the rain
Can anyone say, those two are friends?
Jennifer, with new chores at hand,
helping all others,
Not reliving over sad pasts
Jennifer, with the green-blue eyes, I'm so happy
You look into mine,
Do you see better living? Do you see better ways
Are you just wanting to "git", or make an effort to this?
Do you go back to old ways, even though they lead where?
It really just leaves you waiting back here.
So, as you try this easy new way, does it help you
Live and see things your wonderful days,
You know going back can end this again
Jennifer with the green-blue eyes, won't you live in this truth,
For there will be someone for you

Just an observance

In a bowl stands a crowd formed by an ancient volcano, musicians playing on a stage. Just an observance from the rim, I am standing out to just gaze.

Children dancing playfully, parents watching while they rest, in short folding lawn chairs, blankets strewn out protecting picnic food, drinks and small pets.

Bright sunshine lights the area, shaded by the trees with their towering heights. Gentle winds make their pointed tops flow, a flock of birds have just taken flight. Blue skies frame this picture, green lawns cover slopes of brown dirt and boulder blocks, cement steps form two pathways, a ramp turns a one-eighty, for wheelchairs, people with crutches, or for those who just can't walk.

Through flowing music of jazz sounds, a blowing of a flute, drums tap and sound out rim-shots, brassy sax plays a solo, next to a woman with a lute. Electric piano accompanies slow steady sound of progression played, leading us down and up his wavy funky scale, plucking his giant upright acoustic bass.

The singer sits so pretty, on her stool in front of a mike, performing out to the walking crowd, some have come here on their bikes. Colors mix, venders sell cooked food, smoke fills into our midst. Swells of people just flow about, walking or sitting with their friends.

More people wander from the parking lot, joining an ever engaging throng,
Standing and clapping the musicians, as they start another song.
Gazing at all these people, listening to the jazzy sounds, I'm amazed at all these people, enjoying this summer in this volcanoes crown.

No ticket takers are in the audience, this event is for free, but donations are always welcome as the players often plead. Announced on several occasions, buckets fill with dollars and coins, festivals will continue for more sunny days, during summers long concerts for aficionados' of all types to join.

Let Me Know

Let me know, every once in a while,
every now and again, you make sure,
in both look & words, you have it over me.

Remind me so I see, not that you have the better of me.
I don't know, I just don't know
Not to be smart, but mindful of ourselves,
You & I to others,
To us and others, but mostly for each other.

Don't give yourself permission to do something bad,
Don't let my mind give permission, to think or do, or say, make you sad.

Help me separate the science from the fiction,
And thanks for keeping time set aside,
and for making time for this moment,
to sit watching seas of colorful flowers,
the green shades of trees all around,
And spend some time by the fresh spring,
Flowing now, as it always has before.

Just let me know, every once in a while,
Every now and again,
That you know I love you and you love me for all time, for infinity.

Blonde

Looking over on that small hill

Your hair gently blowing, the wind like a puff

And slightly flowing, your smile growing

With that lovely look in your eye

Can we both look up to the sky?

Broken Bridge

Love should last a lifetime, not held by one but two

Kindness has left your blue eyes, when I gaze out towards you

I always seeked approval, but you never gave it a thought, and you showed your appreciation, by taking a walk. So I'm left here feeling empty, and am standing on my own, no comfort or affection, just here living all alone.

A new morning starts out quiet, just a start to another day, just me looking in the mirror, just me looking at my face. Did I fail to show you something?, Did I make us fall apart?, that the few moment's spent together, hurt you deep down in your heart.

That for you it seems much better, to live your life apart from me, and regret that fleeting moment, when I was on a bended Knee. Many say "if your not happy", it's best to walk away, instead of hurting yourself further, just stop crying like the pouring rain.

One day, maybe tomorrow, they say a change will happen soon, but I don't think we'll be together, I'll be alone now without you.

I guess I missed the steps of loving, as we journeyed on our way, these things I missed in telling, each and every day. My day's and night's need to be positive, as they hopefully are for you, but regardless how I'm feeling , I see our life is though. I'll always be in love with you, as I smile thru my tears, if this is what makes you happy, it will be the future of your years. Then go away my darling, life is short to really care, to take some time to reconcile, make an effort to make repairs. You said that you were broken, from a love loss in your past, and need this time alone to sift and sort, not take another path. To you it seems much easier to leave me, no words of kindness or comfort could I expect to give, to bring us back together, and mend this broken bridge

Me, Too

She loves warm bright sunshine, ripe red berries
From a farm, looking at houses, feeling the touch of
My hand on her face, me, too.
I know what you mean, and as it is,
As always, me, too.

You are what is meant to be, going together thru life.
Lovely days and warm nights with a cool breeze
Embraces of love makes you feel good, me, too.

Hold me close as we sit in the meadow, she
Looks at my eyes and grins such a beautiful smile
She speaks softly and clearly as to say, me, too.

And love is good for her, and love is good to me, too
That there's more don't you agree & so much more ahead for us, she
said with a hug, and heard spoken in her soft, little pink ears, he spoke
Low in deep tones, yes, me, too yes me, too

A sense, concern or worry? Better caution when
Prepared, the end is only the beginning; I nodded, me, too.
Want to walk on the beach today? me, too
Have some waffles your way? me, too
And fold your hands and pray? me, too

You know that I love you, me, too,
As we look eye to eye
And share a smile upon our faces
Holding on to each other tight
With arms that wrap and fully hold as our legs entwine
And up from her ankles to her kind upturned chin
We are comforted to know it is to Him praise the Lord
That gives us peace in you and me, too.

There's a lot of things like, kissing and holding you tight
And she says she likes see my face in the twilight's final shade
Me, too, my love, me, too. Let's prove it, me, too.

Your bunches of lovely things that you do, and smile and
Wink at me as if to say, me, too.
My American wife of God, I make her smile, me, too
Eyes spectacled blue and lips so sweet.
I always knew, we two would meet,
Didn't you?
She smiles and speaks, "Me, too"

My experiment

Static vibes of pent up ambitions

Wires and spools wrapped of blue flashes of fission

Lightning and thunder light up the night skies

Black backdrop dotted with star light and moonlights bright white

Boiling bubbles in liquid filled beacons

Red, green and clear they seem living, yes awaken

Sounds of their rising rattle my instruments and containers

Howling out of the mist makes the night so much darker

My experiment's end is nearing completion

Cardboard and paper Mache mixed in a human figure

Chicken wire holds back my mysterious mission

Crackling and snaps in the lab now grows shriller

My vision of the future begins to shape up this thriller

Springing to life with a sudden jerky drive

My creature is beginning to breathe, it's now coming to life

Twitching with slowness and a terrible movement

It sits up and sways towards me feeling for inducements

My experiment is scarring me

My Mate

Wandering in dark woods dirt and fir needles lay
paths between green moss and brown bushes,

we run amongst trunks of scrub and older tall trees,
on our feet with soft pads that are cushioned.

Light of sunshine peaks through small spaces
of covered branches of small saplings

Shadows darken down towards the crick we
hear faint sounds of water splashing.

Rocks and brown mud and white foam bubble's flow,
over fallen logs among pebbles my mate and I go.

We stop and lick water by the edge of flowing
water so fresh , clear and cold,

filling our mouths satistisfied I look round to
make sure we are safe and our belly's are full.

As we run up the bank brushing leaves and small branches

We see a larger path clear with smooth ruts,
neither one wanting to take chances,

Sunlight lights up our path, gazing out at each other, both
of us stopping to look past fallen trees that give cover.

Ahead we run together, though gusts of fine dust ,
getting split by a beast of black wheels rolling past us.

My mate, in the ditch, is still and eyes are wide
open, yet not a movement is there to be seen

Looking down I see a fly buzzing, or is it a bee?

Whiskered nose knows no twitching,
gazing sideways towards the sky,

Legs still, tail matted, tongue hanging out
of her fangs, bloody nose, bloody hide.

I nudge her to no avail, soft fur splattered in red,

Silent wind blowing along settling dust, my
mate is now still, she surely is dead.

I run in the woods as I slowly look back, searching
for movement from my mate, but her body
lays quiet, her companionship I now lack.

I hear crow's now cawing, from up in the sky, scurrying over
the ditch I hide in the woods, my mates gone and I cry.

At one time

My Megan, my flower, my wife
My woman, the rest of my life

No one seems to care

I'm standing here all alone now, just here standing on my feet,
In the middle of the sidewalk, on this damp and old cement street.
I 've stood here thinking all day, I have thought to myself so hard
How did I get in this position, why has my sweet woman broken my
heart

Can anybody see me, does anyone understand
This feeling that has hurt me so deep, left a stain on my mind like a
brand
I don't know how I might have hurt her, no explanation was told to me
I think back on these past few weeks, to see what problems were to her,
it seems.
I must had done something terrible, I must have hurt you and broke
your heart,
I must had left you feeling, that you could no longer take it, so we
finally came apart.

The relationship has broke down, yes it's broken that's why we split
Even though I've told you, I never cheated or used my open hand or
fists.
Was it caused by mental anguish, did I say I loved you too much?
That I missed you during the day, and wanted to kiss and give you
gentle embracing hugs?

I wanted to spend some quality time together, taking time just to ourselves,
Go out and have a date night, have you call me during lunch.
I see that you didn't want to, no, you just stayed alone to yourself, or spend some time with your Mom and Dad, like I had been placed upon a shelf.

But as I stand here hurting, watching all foot traffic that walks by
No one seems to care for or about me, I am left alone here to wonder why.
No one seems to care or wonders, they don't see that something's wrong,
Yet they'll help anyone else who needs it, begging coins from night till dawn.

Or of course if someone get's physically injured, or has gotten lost out on the street, or has a need for hunger, they want to help get them back on their feet.
But to me that had his emotions bruised, and his ego screaming yet ignored
They just go past me without any help to see, or lend a hand, because my heart has been ripped and torn.

Yes I must have done something horrible, lost a trust you had in me, or didn't show enough attention, no appreciation towards you it seems to be?
Or was it lack of gifts, like the rose I placed in our vase, when you came home to have your dinner, with everything clean and in it's place?

Am I to blame for being attentive, was I smothering you with my love?
What would had happened, if twin children were blessed to the both of us?
Would you have called them needy, clinging for your love and care?
Or would you just abandon them too, not being around to go out somewhere?

You got all your satisfaction, from that job I helped you get, with that new job and profession, where all your needs were met,
With everyone's formalness, manners and your perfection all combined, you didn't separate it to give your family, when it was needed at that moment of time.
You claimed that you were tired, you said it right out loud, but does that mean you couldn't smile, or at least show a little affection, when you finally came around?

So not only do I stand here, empty and lonely as I can be,
as all these people just walk past me, not being a human giving love, do I have to go begging on my knee's?
I stand here feeling lonely, just puzzled and alone as I can be, no one seems to care, won't someone please help me?

But I see that you too have your problems, not really caring to what goes on, no one seems to care, that's the problem, I guess that's why things have gone so wrong.
I guess I'll go on wanting, a hug that I'll never get, just alone here being miserable, because no one seems to care, as my cheeks get wet.

Two of Them

Ocean waves flowed and crashed near upon
Strong wind swept trees along the shore.
Blue skies polka dotted with clouds of white & gray
Hinted rain with almost daring silvery drops
Salty air amongst seagulls sounds blend
with mightily
Continuing curls of the sea,
white, always white with
Either green or brown, smash the shore below cliffs
Of rocks formed high and low in the sunset's glow.

In our matching jackets two of them huddle, cuddle
And kiss, breathing fresh smells of the coastline's mist

Driftwood and sand, dunes and water filled pools,
Reflect the two of them walking on this their honeymoon

Let's fly a kite my darling, smiles fill the table where
They sit, staring with the pleasure only newlywed
Couples get.

As the two of them kiss & hug so warmly,
The two of them embracing, knowing like the
Waves their lover over time, will always exist
In the mercy of God's good grace
Let's do whatever it takes

Once We Had A Chance

So you said you would be with me forever
You said we'd never be apart
All those days we spent together
Must have hurt you deep in your heart

We looked in our eyes and we wondered
We felt our souls were just one and the same
No need to worry of our parting
Their was no cause to give any shame

Days and weeks past like mere moments
Months and years seemed like nothing at all
Loneliness was a thing of the past
It was like we two couldn't fall

Once we had a chance to live our lives out
Once we had those moments of Love
Once we had a chance to be tender
Hold each other like there was no doubt

Over critical delusions of wonder
Seeing things in a different way
Caught you giving your mind a reflection
Giving way to some anger and hate

Reality entered the picture
Unconditional love gave way to abandoned hope
we lingered as we always had designing our future
but was left hanging by a fraying unraveling rope

Once we had a chance to live our lives out
Once we had those moments of love
Once we had a chance to be tender
Hold each other like there was no doubt

So we sit alone without each other
each one sure that it was just meant to be
trying hard to gather our happiness
smiling though it is hard to breathe

so, do you think of reconciliation
do you want to try once again?
Give that love we danced as two partners
hold each other and make some romance?

I hear you try to be happy to others
I just sit here and cry to myself
Knowing that we both want each other
Knowing that this moment has now brought us down

No more roses or candy or lovely flowers
No more love notes I put in your lunch
No more getting ready for romantic dinner's
No more giving you a long bedtime hug

We could be loving each other so gently
wrapped in each others arms holding tight
gazing deeply in each others senses
caressing and hugging to our delight

My sweet lover, now it's over
You are so distant and silent to me
The love that we had for each other
Is now just an old fleeting dream

once we had a chance to live our lives out
once we had those moments of love
once we had a chance to be tender
hold each other like there was no doubt

Paper cut on my eyelid

Spent half of my day, just waiting for you to show

Wondering where in the world you could be?

I borrowed another's phone, just to reach out to you,

Disappointed to no avail, you're not re text'ing or returning my call.

Trolley bells ring as the train clangs on by, like a paper cut to my eyelid,

Tears are swelling, too late I realize.

Wading thru the spattering throng of walking figures, being alone is my fate,

A helicopter fly's above, sounds of feet pound the bricks of the street.

And the hour keeps passing as I smoke my cigarettes,

Fumes blow around blue in the wind like a wisp.

I keep dreaming thru the clouds, of our moments spent in bliss,

And soft skin and our limbs, entwined with our sweat, mingled smells of love rise, mixed scents of sandalwood and rose petals, hold a lasting embrace of long passion, the mattress springs squeak ;under sheets of linen.

A truck rumbles by, awakes me from my dream,

I suck down my coffee, flick my ash under the chair, and drag on my next cigarette. Pink short haired lady, who talks loud to her friends, muffled in sounds of clanking wheels of the streetcars, that roll thru this town, on the tracks, in this heat.

A bi-plane passes over, puffy clouds frame it clear, drifting gray and white against the blue skies, in August of this year.

Sitting here just waiting, skirts swaying from side to side, looking at my phone, it hasn't lit up, or the smile of seeing your eyes.

I want to jump with glee, as we meet up in this place, not waiting like a sentry standing payphone, rub my paper cut eyelid, in my pain.

Pilgrims

We waited 7 years, to embark on this long ocean voyage, traveling with our wives and family, Religion was our vision, a golden sun our guided light.

Thru a few mighty storms, as we headed out west, a journey was set , charted waters almost unknown, with heaven's guidance we went.

From the lanyards a sailor swiftly climbed, on the yardarms high above, a signal from the crows nest, "land ho" was a noise we finally hearkened from billowing sails high atop.

A harbor of calm, steady waters we safely navigate,

to a landing on a rock, we now call Plymouth,

from the last portage of England's run on our escape .

Women were hauled over the side, to the small boats below, a few children went along too, living longer for our hopes of a puritan future's pride. Wayfarers we were, strangers in this blessed land now well kept, we kneeled to our knees, to the Lord our eyes wept.

We gave our good faith, we had traveled a mighty sea, men and woman landing here, giving thanks in a gentle breeze.

We set out to build sturdy homes that were well made, hewn with logs from the woods, we settled knowing winter was on it's way, this place was fine, it truly was good. Thatched roof's covered gable's, fires smoke blowing blue rose above, not knowing who lived as a native nearby, a wall of pointed tree trunks surrounded us.

Our homes by deep forest's, a clearing we made, to sit at wood tables, a meager feast had been laid.

Not much did we have, for no crops were well grown for all of us, we worried that this winter, that it might not be enough.

Some friendly local natives, with baskets in tow, brought meat, fish and waterfowl, a vegetable called maze, some roots, and some wild turkeys all plucked.

We invited them to join us, gathered with us together to give thanks, holding our hands in a clutch, we all sat at the tables, to pray in thanksgiving, to the good Lord above.

Pokie Dots

Pokie dots, pokie dots
White against blue
Pokie dots, pokie dots
I Love you

Pokie dots, pokie dots
Speckled silver and green
Do you know how lovely
you are to me?

Pokie dots, pokie dots
Neon orange and pink
I think you know why
I smile when you speak

Pokie dots, pokie dots
Purple set against red
Pokie dots, pokie dots
You have gone to my head

Pokie, dots, pokie dots
Sherbert aqua over yellow
Pokie dots, pokie dots
I'm so glad I'm your fellow

Pokie dots, pokie dots
Cream and cinnamon brown
Pokie dots, pokie dots
I'm so glad you're around

Polka Dot

Little round balloons taped on a bright white vest
Red, blue & yellow, purple, orange & green pastels
All look so lovely, so joyful all told
The wife is right
Sticky owey gewey
Icky, miss icky
She's a little bit tricky

Set me straight

Time is a place just south of the country of Q.

Where the breeze on the palms makes them sway

And the white lines and soft sounds of the waves

And even though the ocean is blue

The green colors of light and dark

Weave through out till a familiar color

Of blue till the night comes on a new

Ja jamay Jamaica, jaymayceya

Weight Vs Mass

Really, don't take advantage

We're short of time

Man about town, looking around

Sharp, smart

But what does it matter?

What?

She calls it a zam bro,

but I didn't know.

Now she has me eating right out of her hand.

I gave her a glance

and didn't take my chance.

Eyes blinked when I saw & looked again

and wanted to

Remember that look in my sight

Or where to begin

Sleeping Lady

Oh, she lays quiet in curved warmth,

Breathing soft uninterrupted air through all of the night

Her hair, long and blonde curls around the pillow where dreams
tangle amongst visions of past dreams and gone days

Near, her head rests under folded hands
cradling her sweet beautiful face

Soft arms hold tight covers, the clock soon will chime
carrying the sounds to her pretty pink ears

Closed lips smoothly smile as she slowly does wake
to start the bright morning, we share a gentle kiss
to see those light blue eyes sparkle and so full of life

I await

So let the prelude end
And smoothly into our lovely dance of life
Sunshine awakes, stirring dreams of you
With me close, warm & soft thoughts together
Looking into our eyes and smiles ahead,
as we
Take another breath,
I want to dance
And act it all out with you love,

Wanting to show we understand and
Convey together belief and faith all will
Be okay.

Come on Girl, we need to hold each other
Closer and tighter, let's make this moment last forever
And remember each time we get better for
Reflections that linger

These roles we engage to excite is fun
And all I want to do with us always
I await

Tundra

Something to be said for living on
The west side of the river, smell the tundra
And the woods

Something to be said looking to the coast
It's not far, past the beaver dams and all their ponds,
then you climb until you're at the top
Looking out, you see the bay and notice, that it's a
Beautiful day

Something to be said, at the end of the Gorge
Where it rolls in the sea
And the smell of freshness, a smell of
Real life
You can almost taste it in the breeze

Something

It's something, as in the sky,
Something, I can't believe my eyes
Something, a name, a movement, a light

What is it I see, doing gypsy turns
And then goes bye-bye
After rubbing my eyes, from shoddy to superb
All over the tree line ,
yet without a sound
The comings and goings, I guess all around
What is that Something?
Sparkling close to my eye?
When I want to see more, I just wonder why.
Oh something I think, your world and mine
Mix, mix with me closer, or something I visit.
I hope you enjoy your stay!

/

Did you come here to leave it seems to
Believe, that you want to be me & I must say
The same, can we talk & hold thoughts of each
Other?

Home is heaven, heaven is home . . .
Time of life wonders for something to be
Something of this earth
Something soon, yet not believed
My heart knows where I do believe
Now gone so long I hope to see you my friend
But I saw you clearly in the spring day sun
But as yet and I know, it's all about fun
Faster than bullets from a gun I go past the sun
Till you're back to where you've come
You're something . . .

Song Of Sarasota

Sarasota, Sarasota, under morning's yolk yellow skies
Where white sands of Siesta key are so lovely & bright.
Sarasota, Sarasota, palm trees calmly do blow
And the mangroves in the harbors, where the manatees roam.

Sarasota, Sarasota, in the warm Mexican Gulf breeze
Ringling brothers stay here in winter while the rest of us freeze.
Sarasota, Sarasota, I say give it a go
It's so beautiful, you'll enjoy it, on central Florida's west coast.

See the different colored license plates on the backs of many cars,
Makes you wonder, all together, just how many there are.
Friendly faces, vibrant people, see the mission style homes.
Sarasota, Sarasota, now I call it my own.

In the old celery farmlands where the 'gators do grin
Snapping turtles, feathered birds fly, and the marsh tackies live
Sarasota, Sarasota, watching dolphins as they swim.
With my lady, on the shoreline, I shall give her a kiss.

See the masts of the sailboats under the moonlight's bright glow
Baseball players getting ready to be a seasoned pro.
Sarasota, Sarasota, you have given me faith
Sarasota, Sarasota, in Florida's warm sunshine state.

Sunshine

Sun, I'm so happy to see you

Your rays on my face, give me that warm

Embrace

The small layer of thin clouds

Burn off away with your rays, that

Shine, all over the place

I liken you to a woman, you're so

Bright and so warm

Tail of the ring

Church attendants await anticipating the arrival of the groom,
Bride and maidens dressed with flowers, standing in another room
With a ring bought by her father, ready to give her away.
His car pulls up, as he gets out, dressed in his Coast Guard uniform,
debarking from the ship he sailed, now docked in San Francisco bay.

Informed of his presents, the congregation all sits, our priest starts
the wedding vows, waiting to see them both kiss
With two kids from our brides first union attending, they witness her
in her wedding gown. As the words are spoken, we are happy and wish
them well.
They zoom out to go honeymooning, church bells ring out their joyful
noise
Rice is thrown, bouquet is tossed, our couple gets on their way,
We all wave goodbye to them, on their wedding day.

Years go by, the husband dies, our widow lasts for thirty-five more
years
Their eldest son now is getting married, and seeks that ring from his
Mom's wedding past to give to his new blushing bride, it brings his
mother to tears.
He asks for her on bended knee, she says yes, but to ensure that he's
got it alright, It needs to be resized to fit, his fiancée small hand.

A year goes by, it's all in doubt, she asks to go on her own way, selfish independence he mutter's to himself, why did it all turn out ending, how did we get in this place?
He say's not so fast, my soon to be ex-wife, before you decide to leave I want that ring I gave you please, give it back, it's mine, it's not for you to keep.

Weeks go by, the decree is signed by the judge, the ex goes about his merry way, he drives across the USA till he settles in his new home for him it will never be the same.
He sees those rings, he cry's a while, he thinks of what is best for him to do
To sell or hock them is what he decides, and gets a small sum at the pawn shop, like the marriage, it seems kinda cheap.

Months go by, his mother dies, the family gathers and buries her
Then comes to distribute her belongings, they all gather to confer
The subject of the ring comes up, the youngest daughter want that precious ring
He big brother says it's been pawned, she says get it back, how could you do such a thing?

It was mine to do just as I pleased, what if I threw it off a cliff?
She say's but you sold it to that pawn shop, here is some money, go get it for the family to keep.
It's just so sad, that's why it's pawned, but if I ever get married again, I can ask you for it, and maybe this time it will last longer, we laugh.

Taking a walk

Goblets adhere clinging on fine lines of spider webs dusty and old
Mist of the evening blasts with wind of chilly cold
Corner light beams towards creaky steps that look rotten
Rusty hinges holding rails creak with each step I bring on them

Opening towards dark skies an old heavy oak door moves forward with a thud, preparing to enter midnights gloomy misery I start out on my run.
Heavy footsteps crush pebbles with gritty sounds that echo loudly
Shadows dance past light poles of streetlamps surrounding black cats stalking and hiding

Eerie screams of traffic pass thru empty streets and back alleys that I plod
Flashes of bright light reflect on broken glass laying strewn upon dark cracks between grey uneven sidewalks
Out of the corner of my eyes, I see a figure of hunched madness
Twitching in bundles of ragged clothing tattered and smelly grimy psychosis

There in a lump next to this character steaming still on the ground of this lot, reflected in the moonlight I can't believe the glimpse or sight that I got.
A bloody stained heap of humanity lays in a pool of fresh life spilling out , still pouring crimson it drips from the first cut, looks like it's beginning to clot.

In a laughter quite haunting with brutal violent loud coughs
Wicked and turning his dance puts me in a shock
its so shocking and gory, this crazy man dance
But that's not the end to this horrible story's happenstance.

Flashes of broken teeth grinning mad in sweaty secretion,
stubble of his beard covers shred cuts and dried lesions
Hair matted and stringy, humped curves of this figure's back
What could cause me to end up in a violent wicked trance?

Eyes of glee turn towards me, this madman's arm quickly goes up
Aiming for me a dagger flashes from under those rag tattered clothes
Piercing straight towards my being,
I duck and I run.

Going strait for my heart, I step back to keep distance
Tripping behind me I know he doesn't really need a reason.
But from under my belly on my belt buckle safe,
I carry a 22 caliber pistol, and let go of my rage.
He stumble's a step forward, and beginning to drop
Through the loud ring of gunfire, he finally stops.

After speaking to the detective's, and held for a while, they let me go
I continue to go on my evening's long stroll
But as I head to my home of some twenty some blocks
This night has held a story much more than I thought
I've spoken to the papers and those uniformed cops
Now I am home, have a drink, watch some T.V and knock off.

For all that serve us

Thank you, you know,
Just
I can't thank you enough
(for what you've done and how you make me feel)
I'll tell you, I want you to know
You you've got the time for more than a moment
Thanks again. I really mean it
I couldn't pass you by without saying
What my mind just keeps thinkin'
I mean it, deep in my heart
You're the only who cared
To share that look in your eye

And see your sweet smile

I'll tell you, I just want you to know
'cause you make me care or seem to care
thanks again, I really mean it
But Now I know, I wish there were time

Oh how I wish we had all the time it would take

More than a breath, or just a glance,

Or cheeks lifted and firm

And hope I'm grateful, and said it right

I just can't say how you've been in my life

The Banana
and Kitty Cat

Hello fuzzy wuzzy pretty little ball of fur,
And standing right next to you looking like Big Bird,
Is a little bit shiny, and a little bit soft,
The proud yellow Banana with love in his thoughts.

Our Kitty Cat meows then purrs with a smile
Winking her feline aqua green eyes.
As the Banana now wonders if he stands near his prize,
Is it soon or much sooner,
he'll be kissing those lips under cloudless blue skies?

Her tail wraps around him, he feels strong enough.
Her paws stretch out as the Banana curves back, the two are in love.
Their warm lips lock together, just as they both like to do.
And his peel embraces the Kitty Cat's nine lives,
beginning to nestle and coo.

The Banana and Kitty Cat dance away through the day and the night,
Among lush lawns, flowers and tall trees with green leaves,
That flutter, and move lovely, around in the breeze.

Snuggle closer, snuggle closer the two of them hug,
Fragrant wisps linger my blue and white polka dot.
Shades and sun, both enjoy living, both enjoy having fun,
Knowing what they've both got, knowing they're in love.

The Banana and Kitty Cat now ending their day,
Dreaming of just what tomorrow might bring.
Laying down close together, sway away in their sweet dreams,
The Banana and Kitty Cat
Slumber and wonder, slumber and wonder away as they sleep.

Oh so pretty in pastels

The light reflects bright off this moon tonight

And off its glow, my love for you grows

I can see it in your eyes, along with the smile

That shows us why the dream of how we, both of us,

Thoughts join our embrace, and now,

You know we can't wait for the sunrise to begin

A new day, our love, together forever,

Oh so pretty in pastels

The Spanish Gypsy's Guitar

It's traveled all over the world

Made more than a few girls smile

And strings so bright,

The neck to its curls

Sits up right awaiting a master

Oh, play that sound you resound

Three different strums and fingers

That flies over frets like water

Still sits alone in the corner

Longing to be tapped and caressed

And well handled, yet returning in your mind,

As you listen thru the time, of yesterdays

Gone in mere moments,

Blessed to have witnessed the Glory

Those Tualatin Farm Girls

Wonder of wonders, do you ever cease?
Those Tualatin farm girls, the dream of dreams.
Can I hope to see the beauty of your charm?
They maybe good 'ol farm girls but she ain't a Country girl,
come take my arm.

but looking at 'em all, I knew you were the one,
how about you and I go have some fun.

See her walking so fine
Under darkening blue skies,
towards night oh so cool, Blonde hair and legs so smooth.

She dances as gypsy's do
With that certain, um, kind of look
You fill my arms, hold tightly and true
My Tualatin farm girl, your eyes of blue

Her chores of grace just bless the day, I
hope that you and I can relate.
It's nice to know, this cock won't crow until the morning light.
Yet this cock would like to change that chick to a hen.
That thought just runs through my head.
My Tualatin farm girl is mine,
for now and all thru the night

Three words

Compassion, empathy, forgiveness

I forgive you every day, you are a fragile, human being.

Our marriage is yesterdays news . . . But that was once upon a time.

Adults that have failed relationships go though this every day, too.

You may not wish to talk directly to me, why would you?

Maybe one day you will. I feel for your loss of trust in our dreams.

I stand in your shoes as you saw me in my weakness and failures.

As I said, I forgive you for what we did, as I forgive myself on what we lost.

Keep doing what you need to do, as I am doing with my life the best I can.

I understand, Megan, or at least I think I do,

A dream?

Time for warm talk and smiles

Looking at the interest and understanding in our eyes

New laughs and old favorites

Always wishing and kissing and love for each other

A trust in knowing what matters

And how time for warm talk and smiles

Can last forever and always be known

Deep inside where it feels right

And thoughts forward bring joy

And never let tears or sadness upset us so

I never want you to see us let go

Time in the middle

The long ray's of sunshine, announces the day,

blue skies and bird's singing, the bed's warm where you lay.

Measured coffee starts brewing, the alarm starts to ring,

we move to get going, as you put on your things.

But I want to spend some time in the middle, just me and you,

Just a little time in the middle, in the middle , we two.

You've brushed back your hair, we've eaten our
food, we leave in the car, and go for a cruise.

It's time to start work, and get on the phone.

It's one on the clock now, I've eaten my lunch, I'm
done with the dishes, I've vacuumed the rug.

Only four hours to get you, and bring you back home,
and soon we'll be together, we won't be alone.

We can go for a bike ride, throw the ball for the dog, and
gather our night clothes, and snore and saw logs,

It's long since the sun set, and no ones around .

My mind thinks of you love, thru out the whole day, and
now that you're with me, I just want you to stay.

But there's more things to do, to prepare for the week,
visit friends and family, the poetry heard when I speak.

But I want to spend some time in the middle, just me and
you, a little time in the middle, in the middle, we two.

The day has turned into night, the times going fast,
I want to hold you darling, do a delightful dance.

Have we got a moment, to be face to face? Embrace
and entangled, make an end to this race.

And spend some time in the middle, just me and
you, a little time in the middle, just we two.

Now its dark after dinner, with some vocal practicing
ahead, we set the alarm clock, and turn in to bed.

We're tired and sleepy, but as I give you a kiss, we
have the time now, one things in my head, to spend
some time in the middle, the middle with you"

Florida

Splashing against white hang flowing shores as if

I can see the curve of the Earth and wonder

How at a hue of the lights during night

The saw grass blows with a steady disruptive flow

As the roots of the Banyan Tree hold like we hold.

Hug the world today snugly, as when we hug

And kiss and love together warmly, as the sunshine

Returns oh so timely, as heat and brightness

Takes over, and gives comfort as we look in each other's eyes

Tinted colors of a green white hinted with blue ink
The clouds spill silver & white, across rivers of wind
Fill up my mind as I hear the wind sing
Fully and gentle thru the palms a rough grass
State of Florida, I want to come back

To Be Up, And In

Hat duffin' while out on the course golfin'
I saw and played the tee just right to the hole
To be up and in, to be up, and in
Lovely grass of gorgeous shades of green grass moved perfect

Amongst the flowers, scrubs bushes and trees.
To be up and in, to be up, and in
The sky is so blue with a few soft white clouds

And a cool breeze near by.

Can you hear the birds in the air, flying?

Are your eyes sharp and clear on the distance

And focused on this shot?
To be up and in, to be up, and in
Carry me back thru the links again together
Tomorrow my love, and again we will both
Take the walk.
To be up and in, to be up, and in
Oh to up and in

Discipline

Victimize or learn

Do what you're told

Devine intelligence

I saw two gypsy wagons

And they weren't loaded with violins and tambourines

If you know what I mean as I spoke

But being there love to me is priceless

This cock would like to change that chick to a hen

Us

We are the last two standing

Now that the crowd has thinned out

Lingering sounds mix with the lights turned down or off

The stage is so dark now, you can just see the chair

We still can dance together, enough of the
music returns in our thoughts.

Dance with me my partner hold me close don't let go,
her warmth now & forever

I gave you a book, filled full of blank pages
Don't pass it up, it will always hold favors

We can be Happy

Is my phone working? I can see the lights
On there's plenty of juice. It shows fully charged
Don't you have half a buck for the payphone
I think there's one up the block, and when you call,
when we meet we'll be happy, just up the street by the curve
At the top of the hill

Teeth outlined with a smile I try to look handsome
I drive in my old blue sedan and the joy when
We meet, now we drive down the road now
You make sure that you're buckled

Let the pleasantries begin, until the night ends
And my mind is of you, as I wait till we meet
And I know we can be happy

My Megan

We don't pass it up, get enough, cahdunk
Sturdy and dependable,
thru in and thru out the day
My Megan never leaves me,
she always comes back
She returns as she goes,
we two are one always.
It gives love and comfort,
that makes me feel warm
With a smile. Thru to my eyes,
ever there in my mind
Glowing colors in focus,
like an east coast autumns foliage
Against blue skies and crispy leaves
blowing across loudly
The 18mph earth circling the sun in our Heaven
Yes kiss and hug each other often,
even though we will
Never be apart,
with my love night and morning
With her I'm never alone
Till she . . .
Splits from both of us

Fine shoes

Were your Leopards lucky my lady?
Did they swiftly take your thru the close?
Was the fit snug and softly comfortable?
Are the soles steady and sure?

Were your Leopards lucky, my lady?
Sweet smiles glance brightly upon your face.
As you lead, follow, and guide all the day.
Safely on your way to a sale

Were your Leopards lucky lady? Yes!
I can tell in the way that you smile
Clean them at night,
They'll ready and bright
To be worn on another lucky day!

Hum Drum

What do you want for dinner? My Love?
We have salad, and pasta, and beans
Salad, pasta, and beans
And, your choice, of a cold or warm beverage
Be it ginger-ale, peach — tea or milk?
Ginger-ale, peach —tea or milk
And what do you want for dessert, lovely sweetness?
Juicy strawberries just freshly picked?
Red ripe strawberries just freshly picked
Or and ancient recipe mixed up in a bowl?
Mixed up in a bowl

What's that I see?

So I begged for us to communicate, and was answered with nothing but a smile
This I had seen with my own open two eyes, that you and I were drifting apart by miles
You didn't have any difficulty, speaking to anyone, anybody who you thought I would despise,
But to me you clamed up and became distant, found anywhere to run and hide

But when it came to you and I dear, you just filled my big ears with empty air
when it came to enjoying some us time, when quality mattered to be together and near
you answered my request with avoidance, found anything else was more important for you like ice cold beer. That quality time was just so crushing, it brought nothing like love just despair

Drifting apart was a well played out sport now, getting further from me was an art
Time away was more frequent, like a wind blown smell wisp of a fart
You repulsed me during our meetings, made a few uncalled snide acrid remarks
Directed them loud and so clearly
Made sure that you delivered them strait to my heart

No more loving hugs or kisses,
No more deep gazes into my eyes,
No more warm touch or embraces,
No more love reaching out, just a disguise.

So I suppose it is over between us
There's no reason to go on with this,
That from this very moment
Our relationship is in remise

On the day that dissolution became around and it ended
On that day that I finally signed
I saw a smile from you that gave me a chill girl
The sparkle had gone from your blue eyes

but it wasn't me who had ended it
no it wasn't me that upped and walked away
I asked for some reconciliation and forgiveness
all I got was a walk to our relationship's grave

I'm having a ball with the women,
I am having the time of my life
It's so much fun to be let loose
Of that ball and chain thing called my wife

You were holding me back I surmised now
Now it all becomes clear to me
And if holding me back was your plan dear
I'm just glad I have found some relief

You Know How To Train Me

I talk too much, just stop and help me
And to me it would mean so much
To call me Christian, is different than calling me Chris
But I do long to hear you say it, and now, I don't
Hear it so much

I wish you know what this means, and let me
Know now if not sooner

Because you know how to train me
And to me it would mean so much
I talk too much, I think too much
About it

But you gave me the green light,
I didn't think you were kidding me
I just thought, go ahead, go get ready,
And the green light shouldn't be shown

Gal, pal

You're so fine, I want to take the time

Confer that we're going at it right

You're quite a gal, pal

I think about being with you, how you make me

Think about myself, and I try to come up

With things to think about offering you a choice

Oh I hope that choice can come true

I don't like to feel you don't have a choice

Not letting you have to, or make you, or anything

Like that, just smiles between the both of us

How I wish you would take my two suggestions

Or show me the best way to go.

Well, what do you know? Well quite a lot

Openness of framed structure, it depends on the time

I run a foul often

So what would you like,

Or I can make that decision for us both